"Every moment
is a fresh
beginning."

T.S. Eliot

My Old Home

MY FAVORITE PLACE AT HOME

_____
_____
_____
_____
_____
_____
_____
_____
_____
_____
_____
_____
_____

A PHOTO OF MY HOME

WHO LIVED WITH ME HERE?

My Old Home

SOME OF MY FAVORITE MEMORIES HERE WERE...

_____
_____
_____
_____
_____
_____
_____
_____
_____
_____
_____
_____

I will always remember

THE FUNNIEST MEMORY I HAVE AT MY OLD HOME...

THIS MADE ME SMILE

WHAT MY ROOM LOOKED LIKE

Memories: the good and bad

THAT ONE TIME I ACCIDENTLY...

HOW COULD I EVER FORGET

Memories: the good and bad

I WILL NOT MISS

BUT I WILL MISS THIS!

MY OLD SCHOOL:
_____

School Days

AT SCHOOL I LOVED...

_____
_____
_____
_____
_____
_____
_____
_____
_____
_____
_____
_____

CLASSMATES!

School Days

IN MY TOWN I USED TO...

_____
_____
_____
_____
_____
_____
_____
_____
_____
_____
_____
_____
_____
_____

Happy Memories

ALL THE PEOPLE, PLACES, AND THINGS I WILL MISS

Happy Memories

ALL THE PEOPLE, PLACES, AND THINGS I WILL MISS

Happy Memories
ALL THE PEOPLE, PLACES, AND THINGS I WILL MISS

Happy Memories
ALL THE PEOPLE, PLACES, AND THINGS I WILL MISS

Happy Memories
ALL THE PEOPLE, PLACES, AND THINGS I WILL MISS

Happy Memories
ALL THE PEOPLE, PLACES, AND THINGS I WILL MISS

Friends Forever

A NOTE FROM _____

A NOTE FROM _____

Friends Forever

A NOTE FROM _____

A NOTE FROM _____

Friends Forever

A NOTE FROM _____

A NOTE FROM _____

Friends Forever

A NOTE FROM _____

A NOTE FROM _____

Friends Forever

A NOTE FROM _____

A NOTE FROM _____

Friends Forever

A NOTE FROM _____

A NOTE FROM _____

Friends Forever

A NOTE FROM _____

A NOTE FROM _____

Friends Forever

A NOTE FROM _____

A NOTE FROM _____

Real Talk

WHEN I THINK ABOUT MOVING I FEEL...

Real Talk

WHAT I'M MOST EXCITED ABOUT WITH MOVING IS...

Real Talk

I'M A LITTLE ANXIOUS ABOUT...

_____
_____
_____
_____
_____
_____
_____

BUT I'LL WORK THROUGH THIS BY...

_____
_____
_____
_____
_____
_____
_____

Real Talk

ON MY LAST DAY IN MY OLD HOME...

_____
_____
_____
_____
_____
_____
_____
_____
_____
_____
_____
_____
_____
_____

Moving Day!

MY MOVING DAY EXPERIENCE

_____
_____
_____
_____
_____
_____
_____
_____
_____
_____
_____

MY MOVING DAY EXPERIENCE

_____

_____

_____

_____

_____

_____

_____

_____

_____

_____

_____

My New Home

WHAT I LOVE...

WHAT I WILL CHANGE...

MY NEW SCHOOL:
_____

New School

MY FIRST DAY IN THE NEW SCHOOL WAS...

_____
_____
_____
_____
_____
_____
_____
_____
_____
_____
_____
_____
_____

I MET SOME NEW PEOPLE...

_____
_____
_____
_____
_____
_____
_____
_____
_____
_____
_____
_____
_____
_____

"There are far better things ahead than we ever leave behind."

C.S. Lewis

New Adventures

PLACES I WANT TO EXPLORE...

1. _____
2. _____
3. _____
4. _____
5. _____
6. _____

NEW THINGS I WANT TO TRY HERE...

1. _____
2. _____
3. _____
4. _____
5. _____
6. _____

New Adventures

I'M LOOKING FORWARD TO...

_____
_____
_____
_____
_____
_____

MY NEW FAVORITE PLACES ARE...

_____
_____
_____
_____
_____

New Adventures

Dear Journal...

Dear Journal...

Dear Journal...

New Adventures

Dear Journal...

Dear Journal...

Dear Journal...

New Adventures

Dear Journal...

Dear Journal...

Dear Journal...

New Adventures

Dear Journal...

Dear Journal...

Dear Journal...

New Adventures

Dear Journal...

Dear Journal...

Dear Journal...

New Adventures

Dear Journal...

Dear Journal...

Dear Journal...

New Adventures

Dear Journal...

Dear Journal...

Dear Journal...

New Adventures

Dear Journal...

Dear Journal...

Dear Journal...

New Adventures

"Life is a journey, not a destination."

Ralph Waldo Emerson

Made in the USA
Las Vegas, NV
02 April 2025